Clueless George is Watching You
copyright 2006   Pat Bagley
Printed in the United States

editor: Dan Thomas

First Edition

9 8 7 6 5 4 3 2 1

ISBN 0-9744860-6-X

White Horse Books
1347 S. Glenmare St., Salt Lake City, UT 84105
(801) 556-4615

Clueless George

is Watching
YOU!

Pat Bagley
White Horse Books

This is George.
George is a monkey.
George is the president.

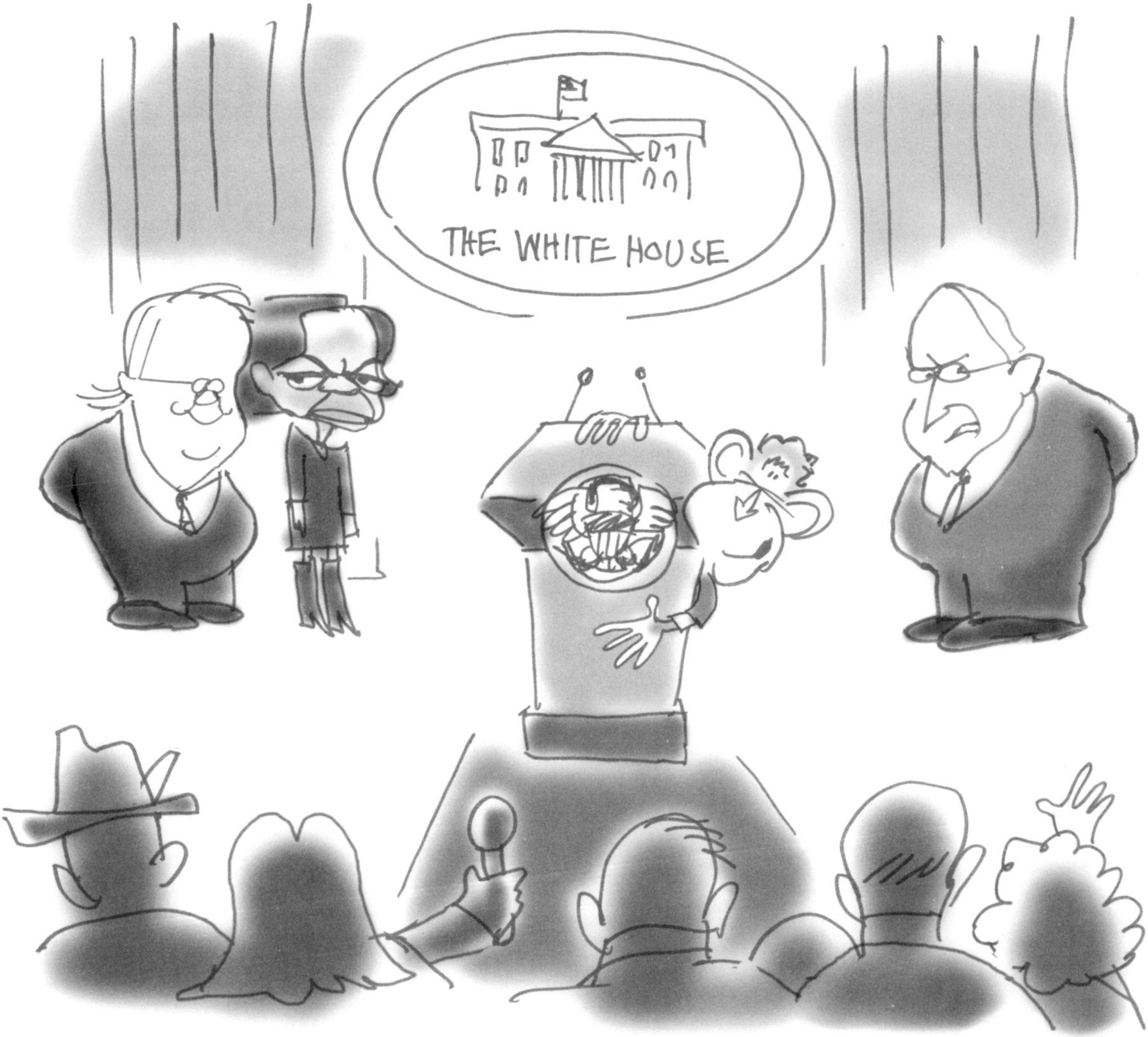
THE WHITE HOUSE

Go figure.

George lives with The Man.

One day, The Man came in looking even grimmer than usual.

"I have grim news," he said.

"They recounted Florida?" George asked with a frown.

"No, not that."

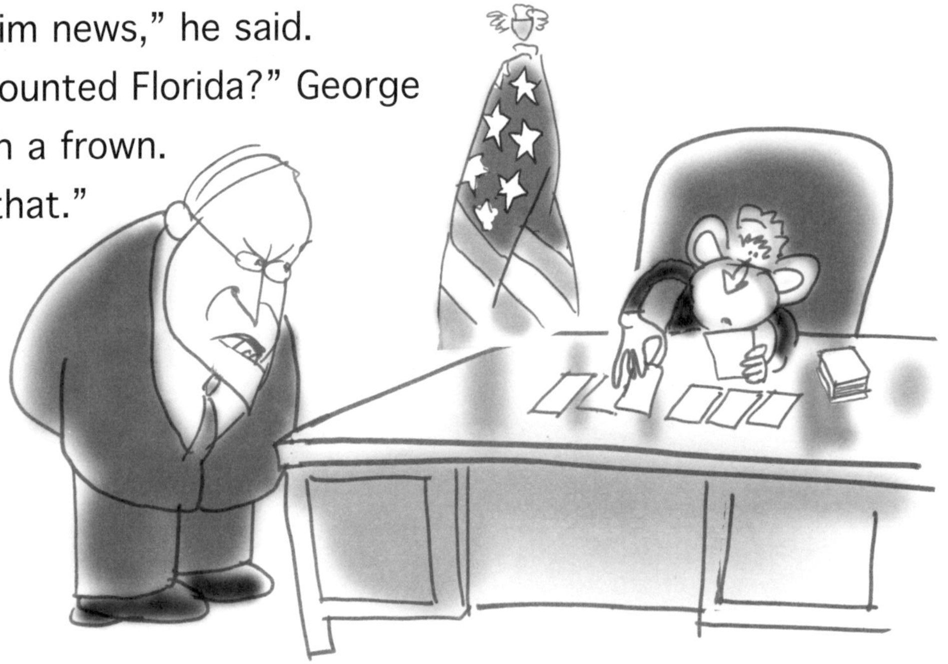

"Men with boxcutters who live in caves are going to destroy a thousand years of Western Civilization and bring America to her knees!!!"

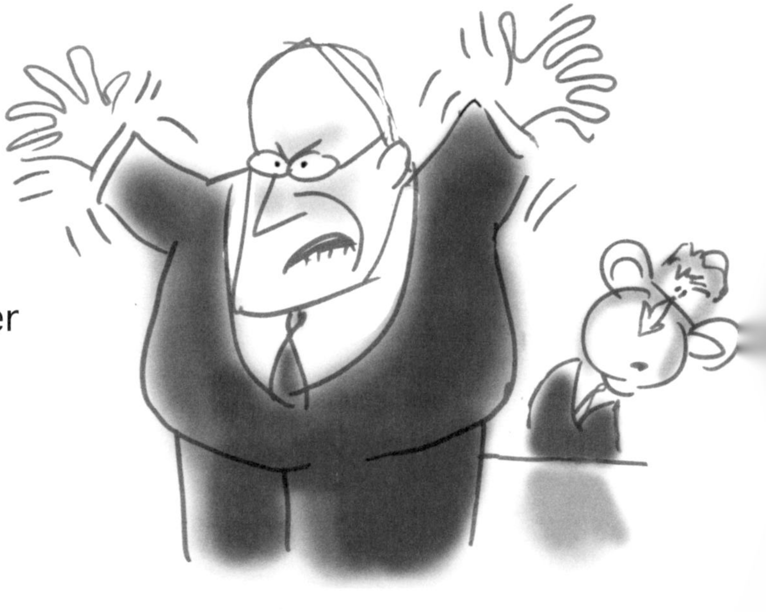

"That is a good one!"
said George.

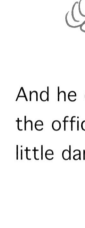

And he capered around
the office, did a funny
little dance . . .

. . . and slapped his hands on the floor
to show that he got the joke.

But The Man wasn't smiling.

"Let me tell you a story . . ." said The Man.

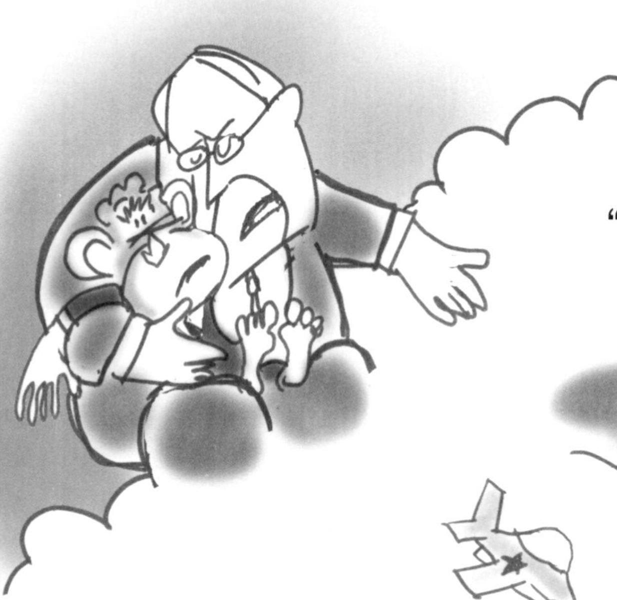

"One day the Soviets invaded Boxcutterstan."

"Hooray for the Soviets!" cheered George.

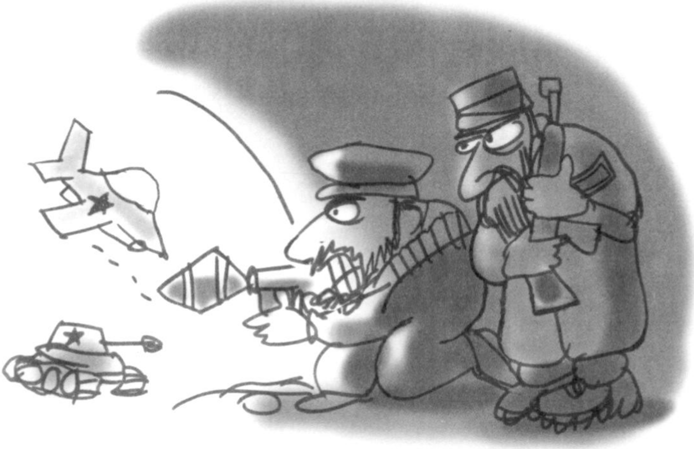

"Wait until I'm finished—Back then the men with boxcutters were on our side and the Soviets were an Empire of Evil."

"I hate Evil Empires," said George. "So we were on the side of the men with boxcutters?"

"Yes," said The Man, "but the evil Soviets called them 'terrorists.'"

"Hooray for the terrorists!" said George.

"We called them 'Freedom Fighters,'" corrected the Man.

George was thoroughly fuddled.

The Man gave up on the story and just told George the boxcutterstanians were back to being terrorists.

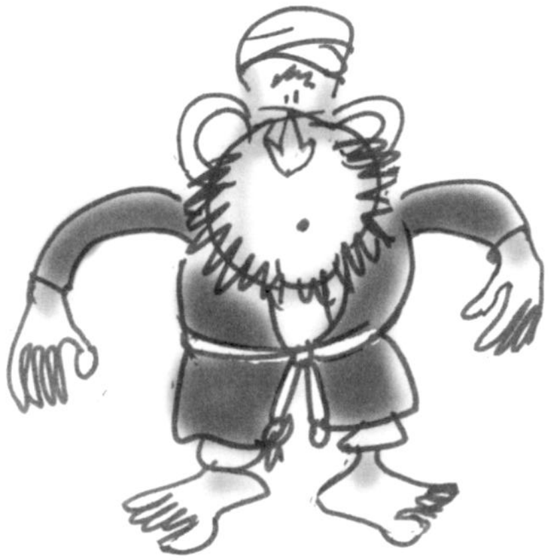

. . . and they wanted to make everyone wear bathrobes and beards.

Except women, who would be forced to dress like ninjas.

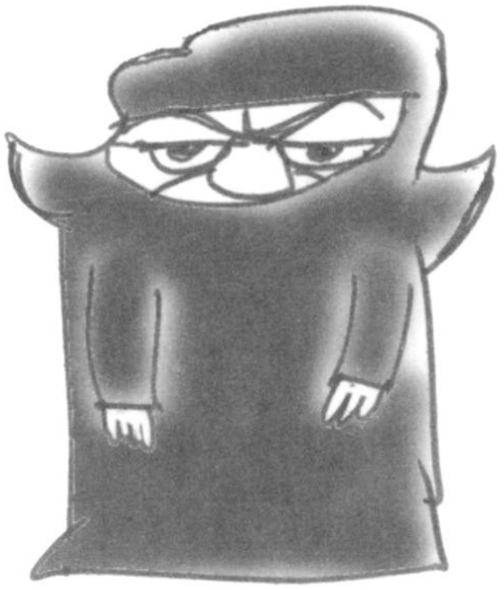

"Even Condi?" asked George.

"Even Condi," said The Man sadly.

And everybody would have to read backwards.

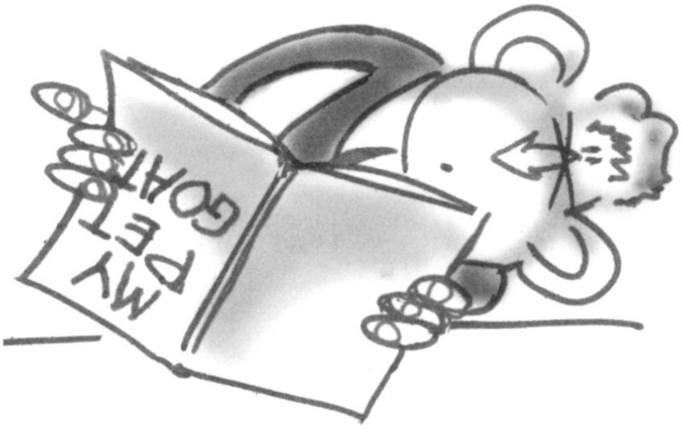
MY PET GOATS

"Reading backwards is wrong," said George. "That proves they don't know the right way to do things. We should teach them a lesson so they do things the right way."

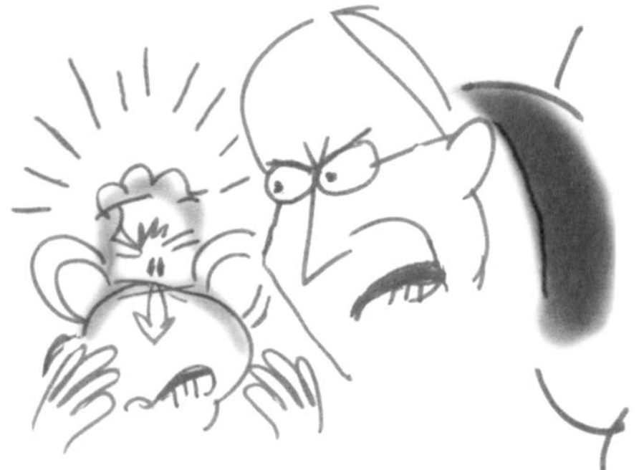

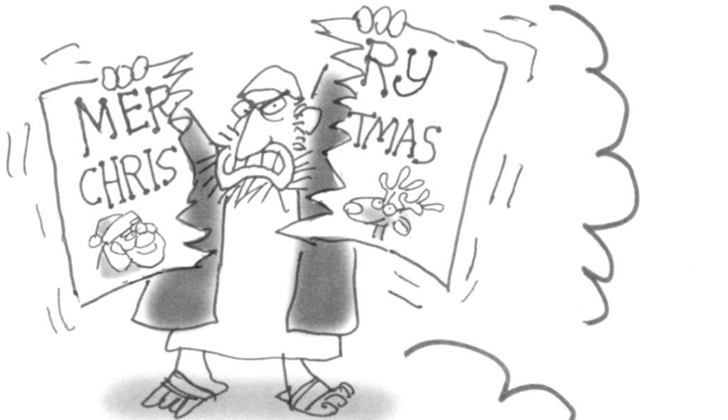

MER
CHRIS
RY
TMAS

"Worst of all," said The Man, "they want to stop Christmas from coming!"

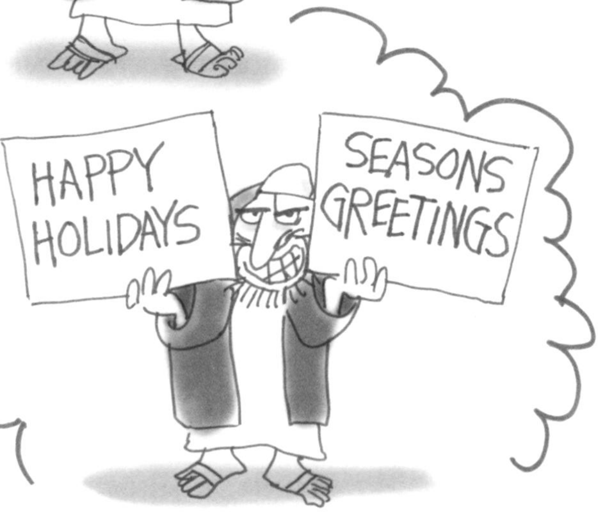

HAPPY HOLIDAYS
SEASONS GREETINGS

"What?!!!" screeched George.
"Those Boxcuttericians are evil!
We must save Christmas!
We must save Santa!
We must save seasonal retail profits!"

"That will be hard," said The Man.
"They could be anywhere."

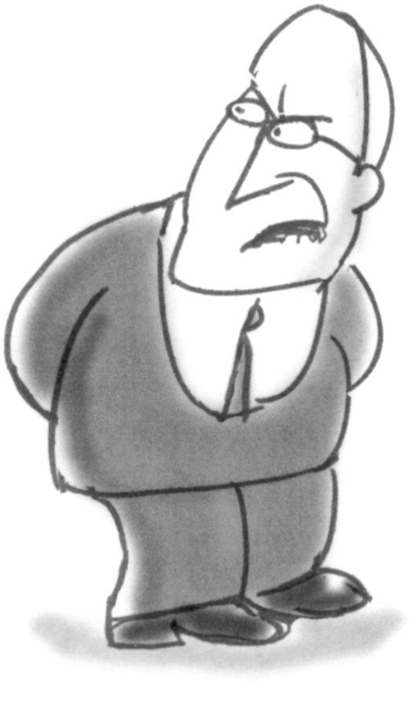

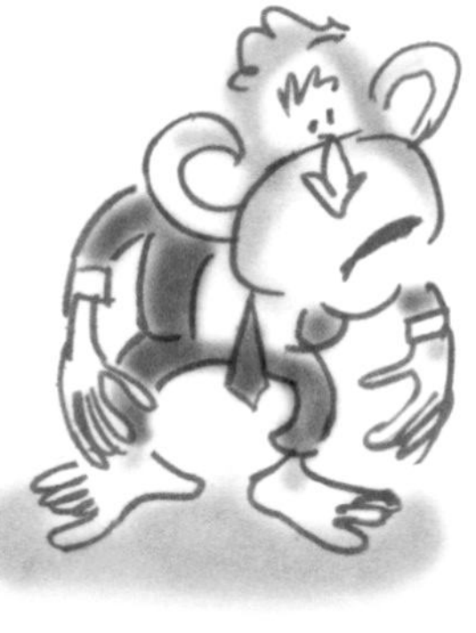

So George looked for terrorists under his desk . . .

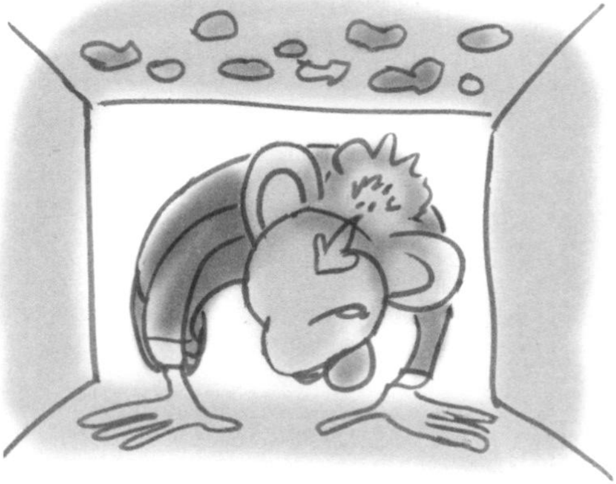

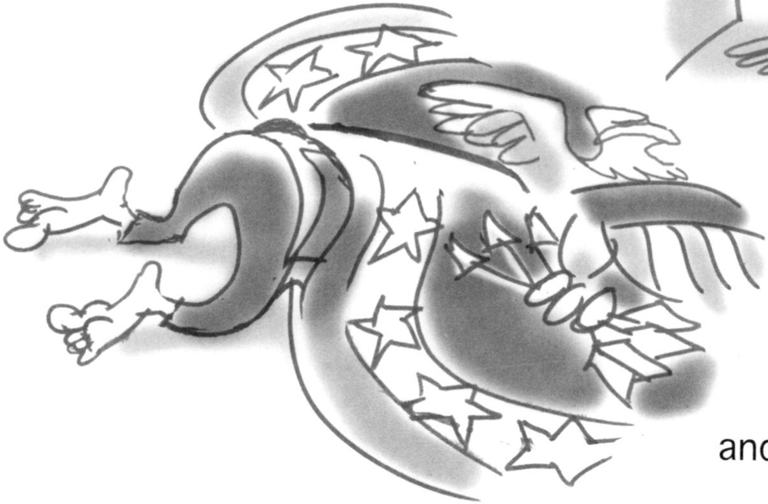

and under the rug . . .

and under the sofa.

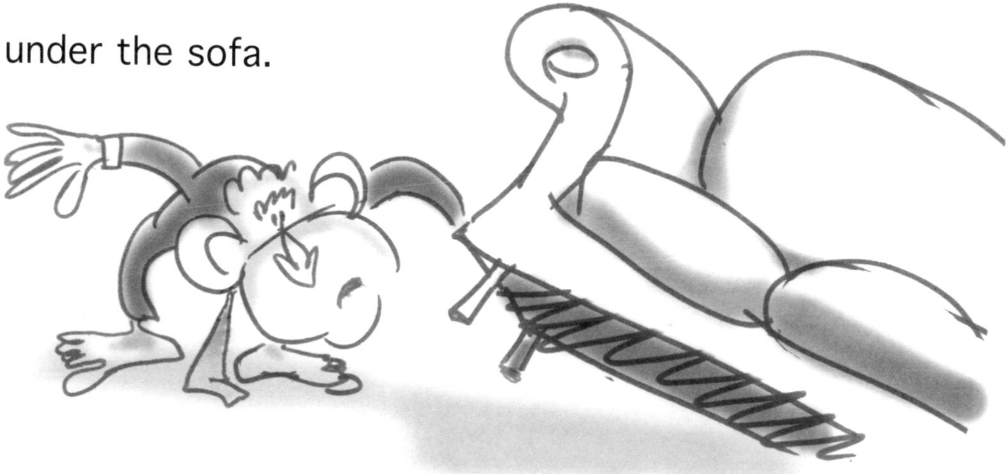

“Looking for terrorists is hard work,” said George.
“Yes,” agreed The Man, “it is hard work.”

“I’m bored,” said George.

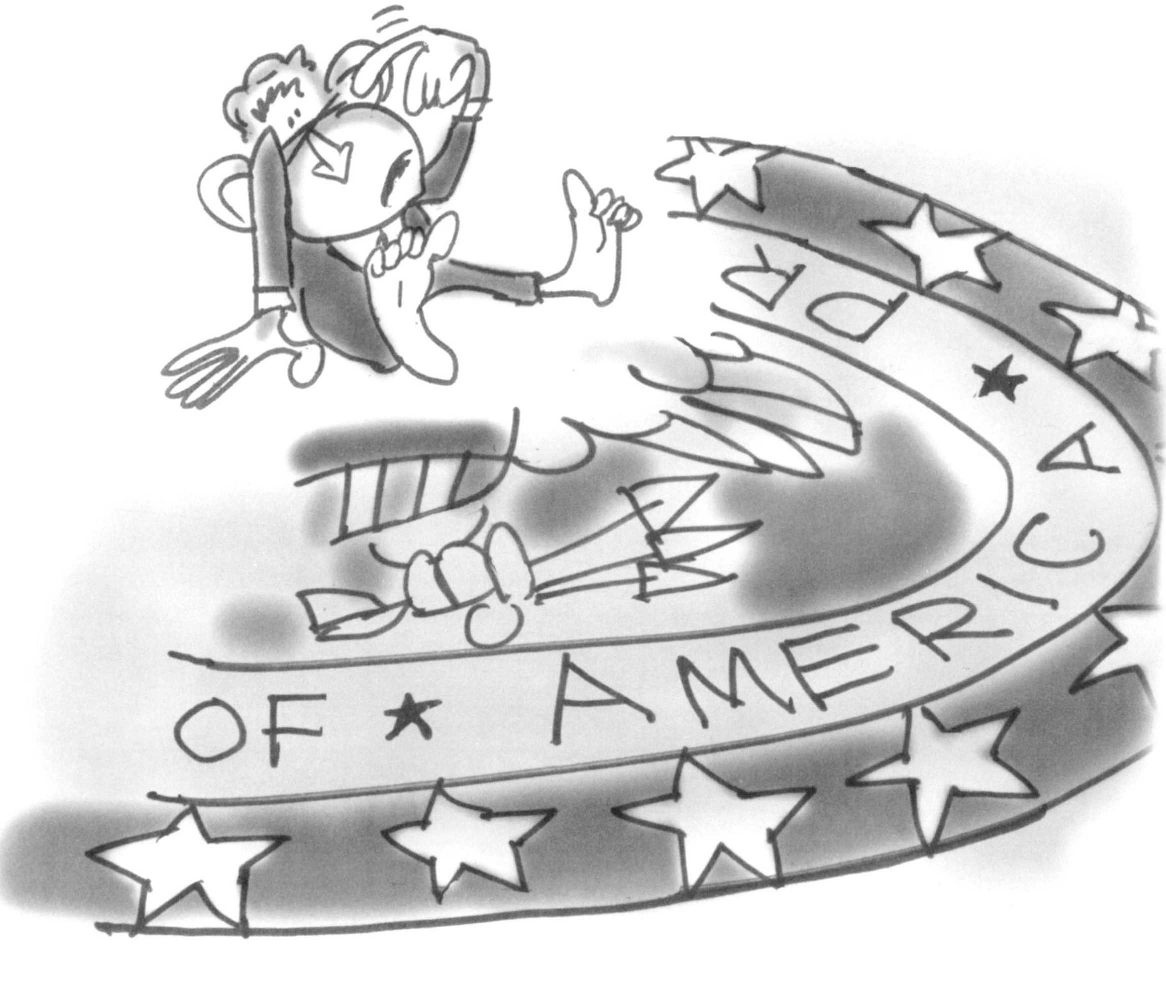

OF ★ AMERICA

"You just need a little help," said The Man. And he pushed aside a curtain.

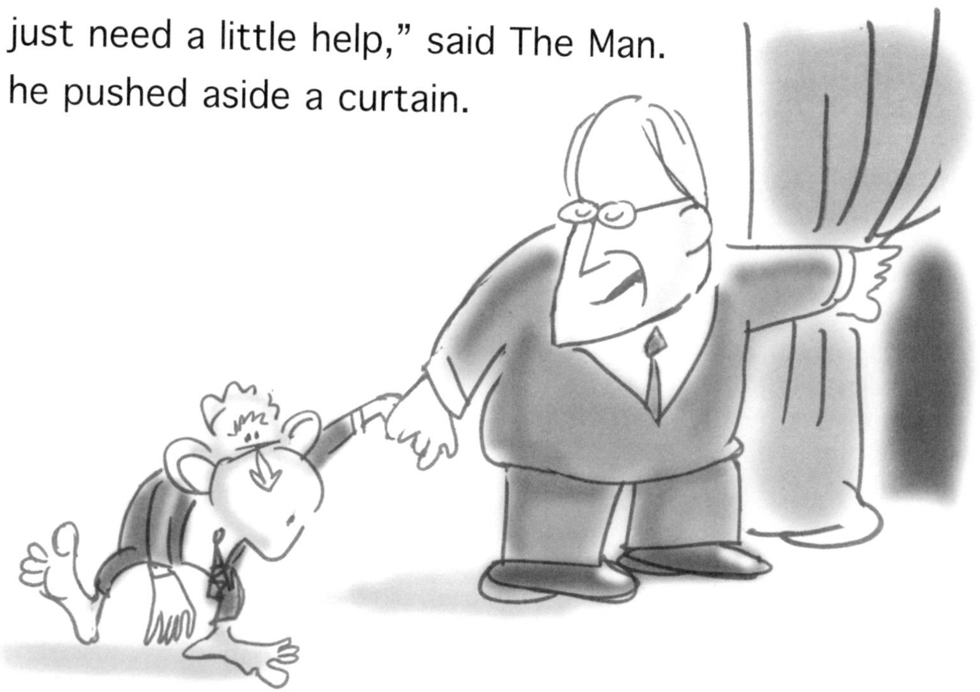

George blinked.

And he blinked.

And he blinked again.

George was dumb-

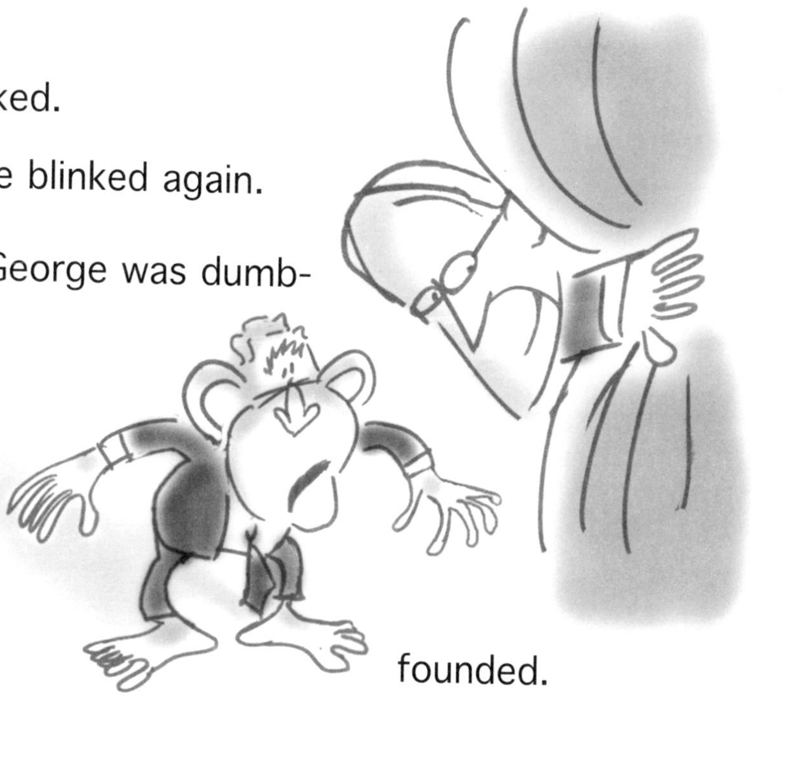

founded.

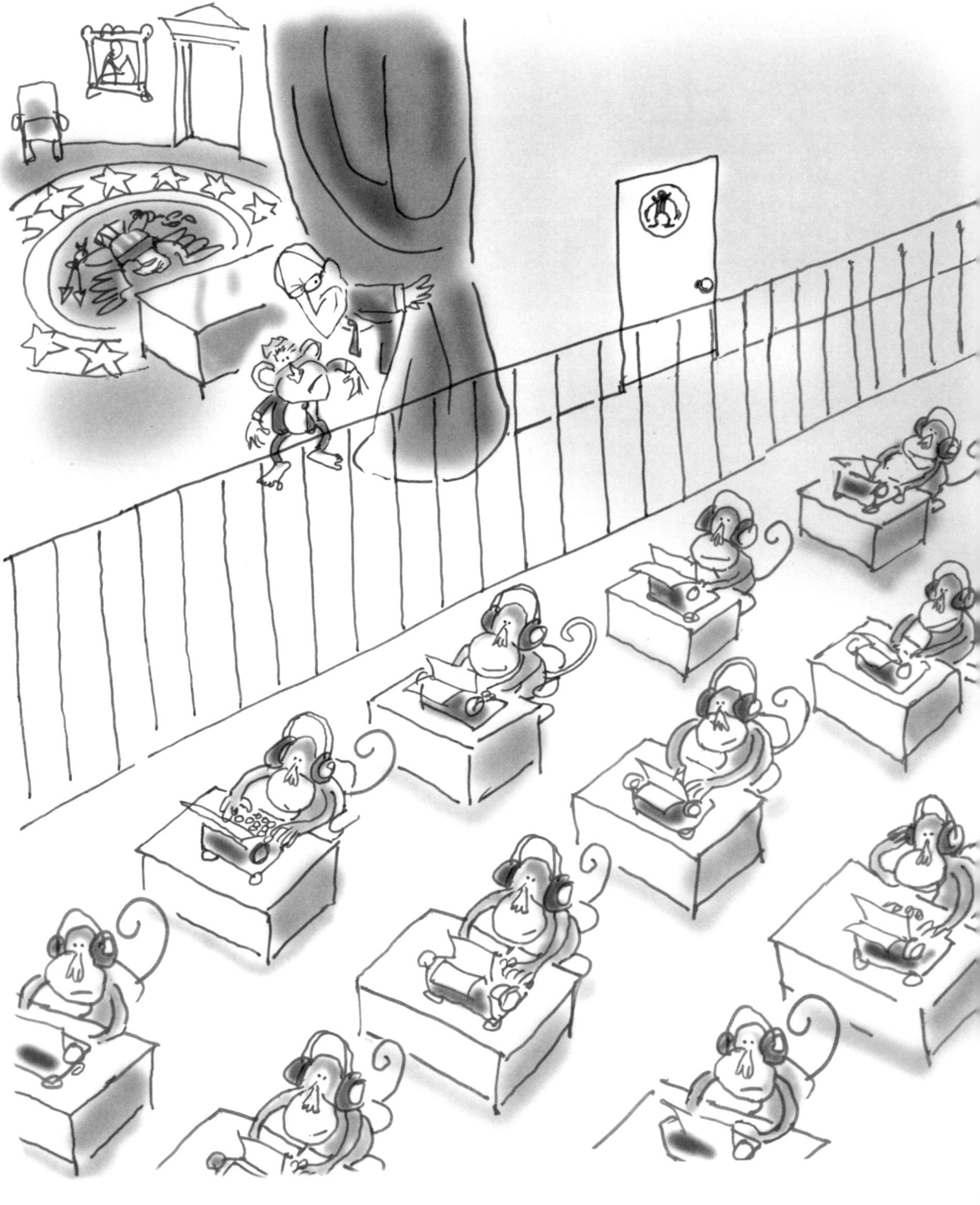

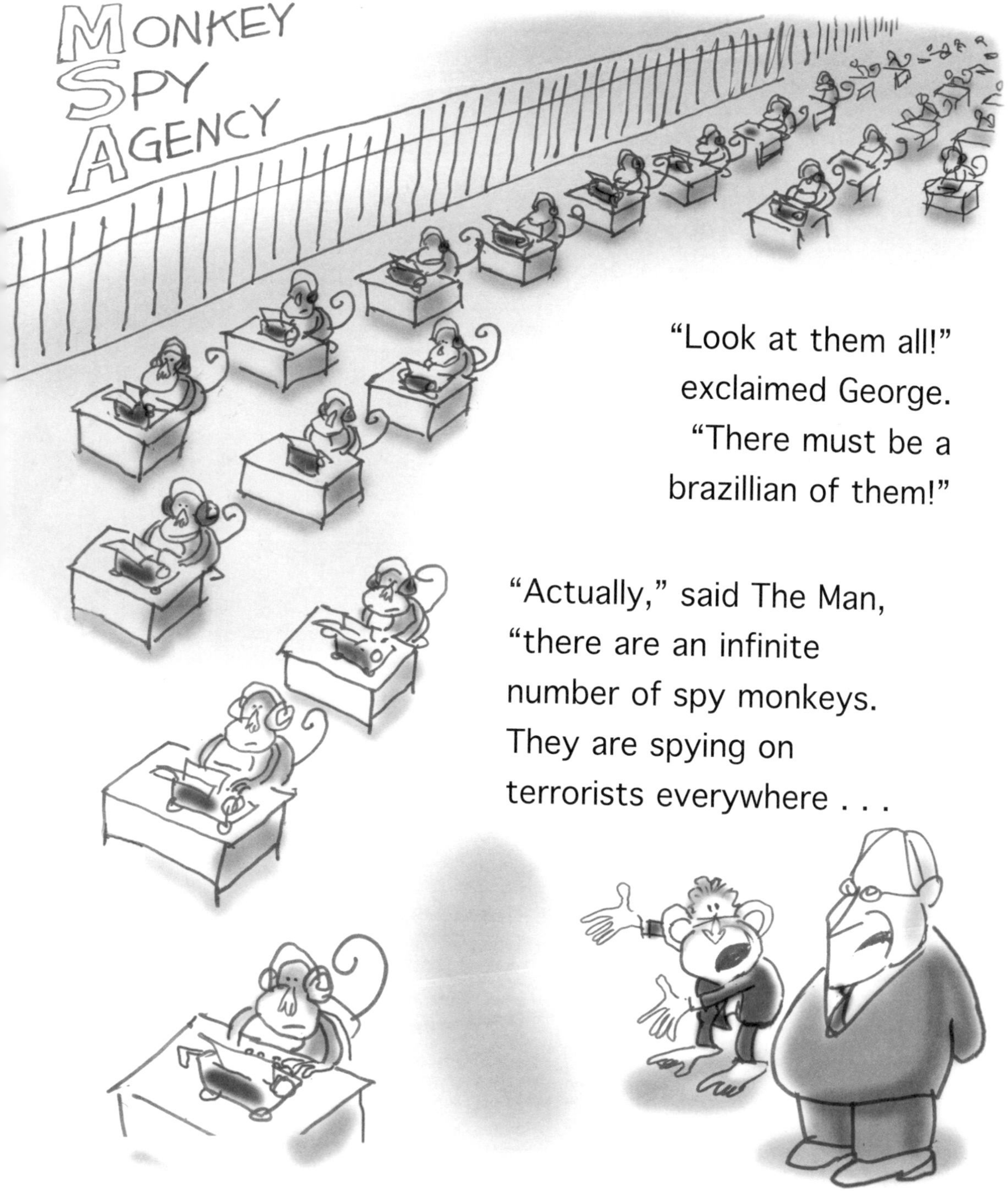
MONKEY
SPY
AGENCY

"Look at them all!" exclaimed George. "There must be a brazillian of them!"

"Actually," said The Man, "there are an infinite number of spy monkeys. They are spying on terrorists everywhere . . .

. . . everywhere but in America."

"Why can't the spy monkeys spy on bad men in America?"

"Because weak and worthless latte-drinking liberals say there are rules against that."

"That is stupid," said George.

The Man sighed. "It is too bad we don't know a wise and good ruler who can ignore stupid rules."

"I know! I know! I know!" said George excitedly. "I could be that ruler!"

"Okay," said The Man, "but let's not tell anyone."

"I am your Ruler Monkey!" proclaimed George. "You have to do what I say!"

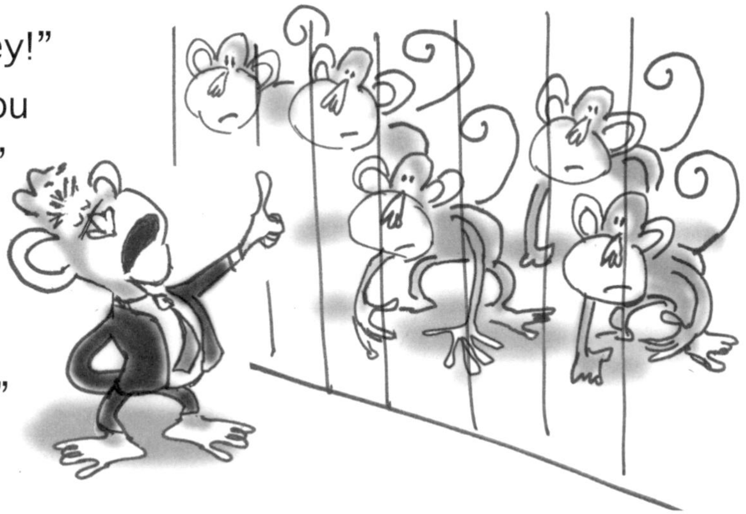

The monkeys all said, "Ruler Monkey says, spy monkeys do!"

"Good!" said George. "Now go look for terrorists in America!"

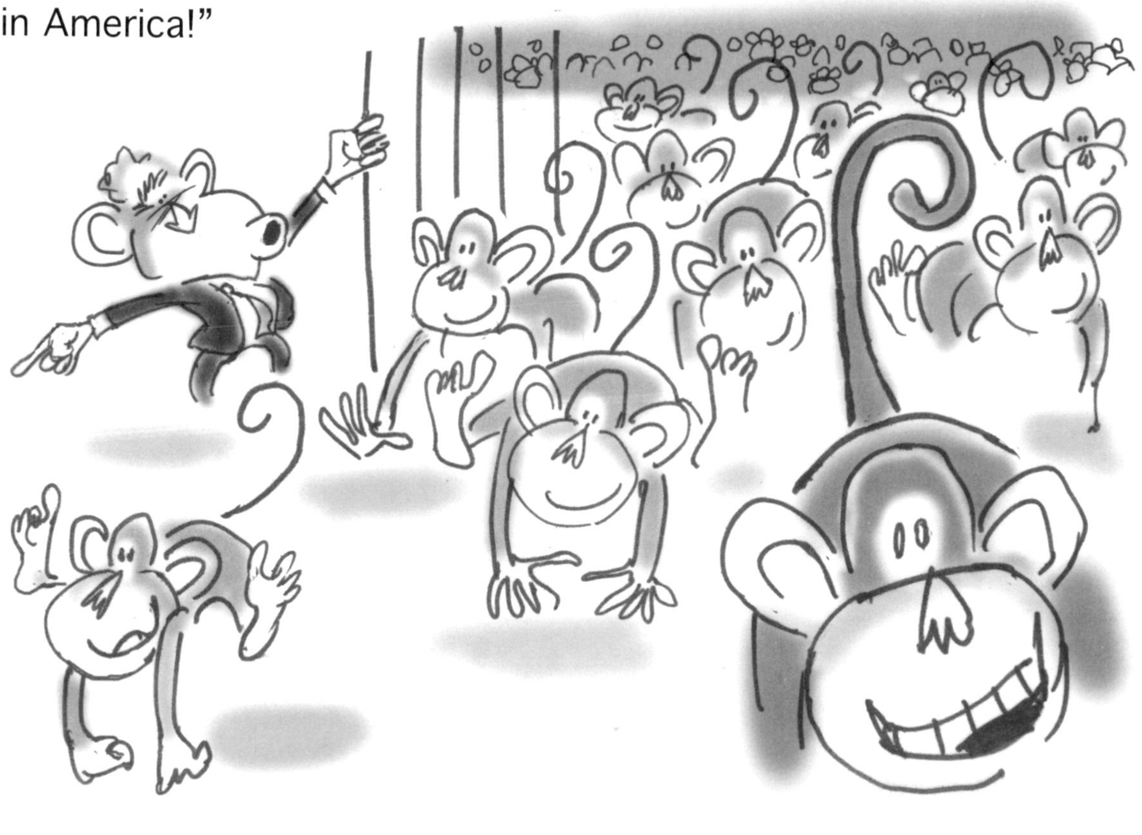

But there was one monkey named Winston who didn't go.

"It is against the rules to spy on Americans," said Winston.

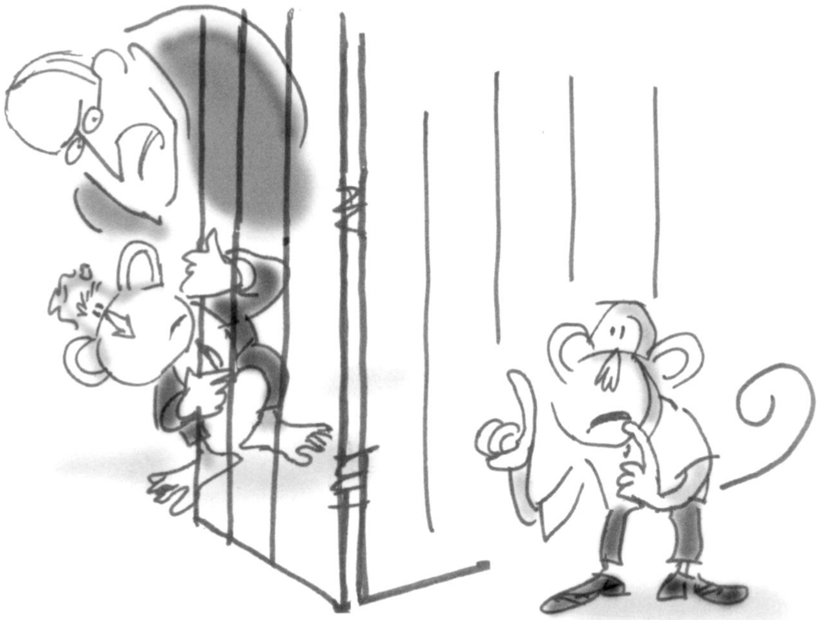

"I am the Ruler Monkey and I say it is NOT against the rules," said George. "You are a latte-drinking liberal!" and he shut the cage on weak and worthless Winston.

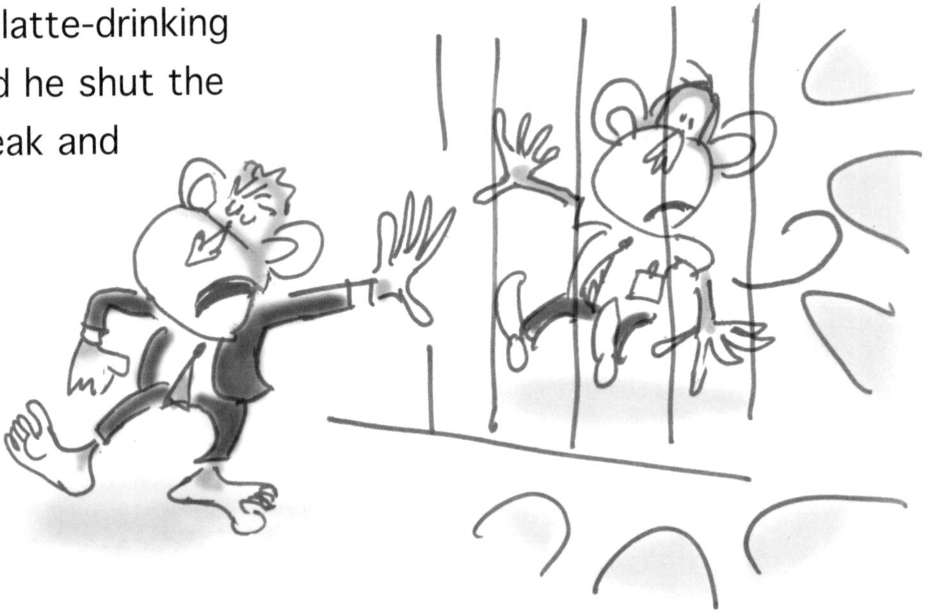

In no time the spy monkeys were looking for terrorists everywhere.

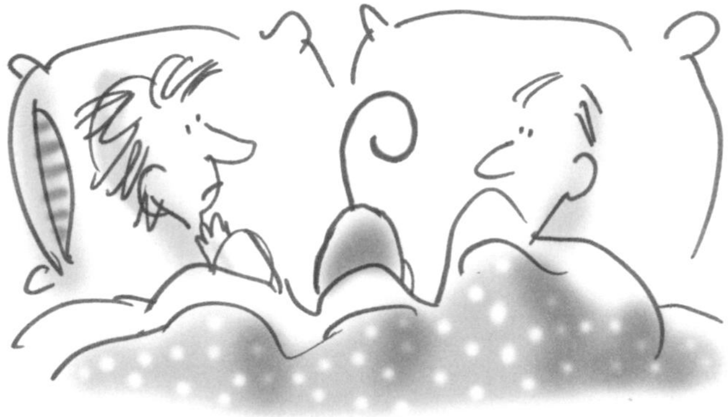

Some went undercover . . .

Others looked in offices . . .

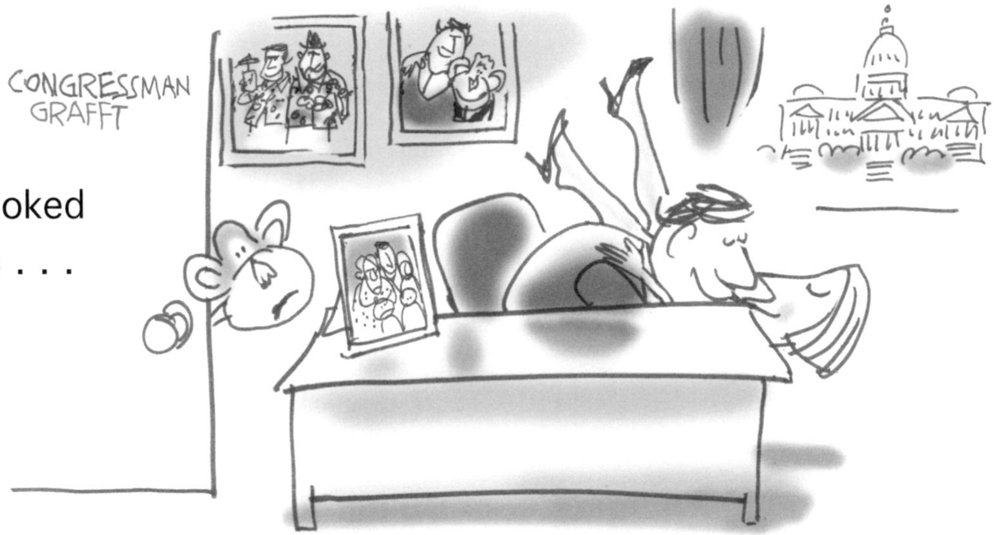
CONGRESSMAN
GRAFFT

and behind benches . . .

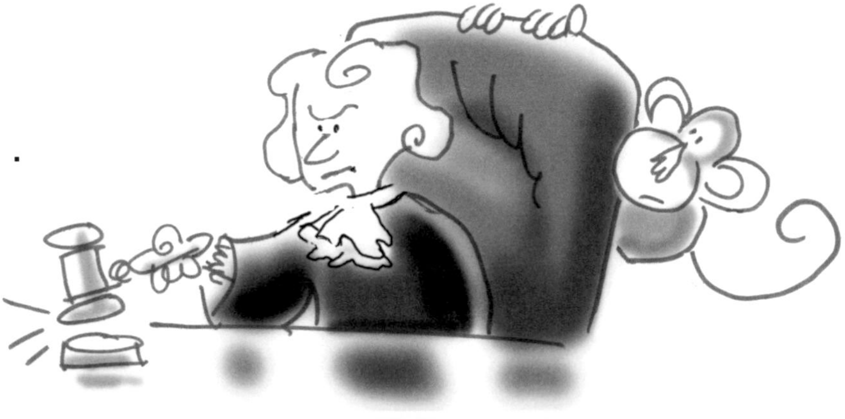

. . . and in closets.

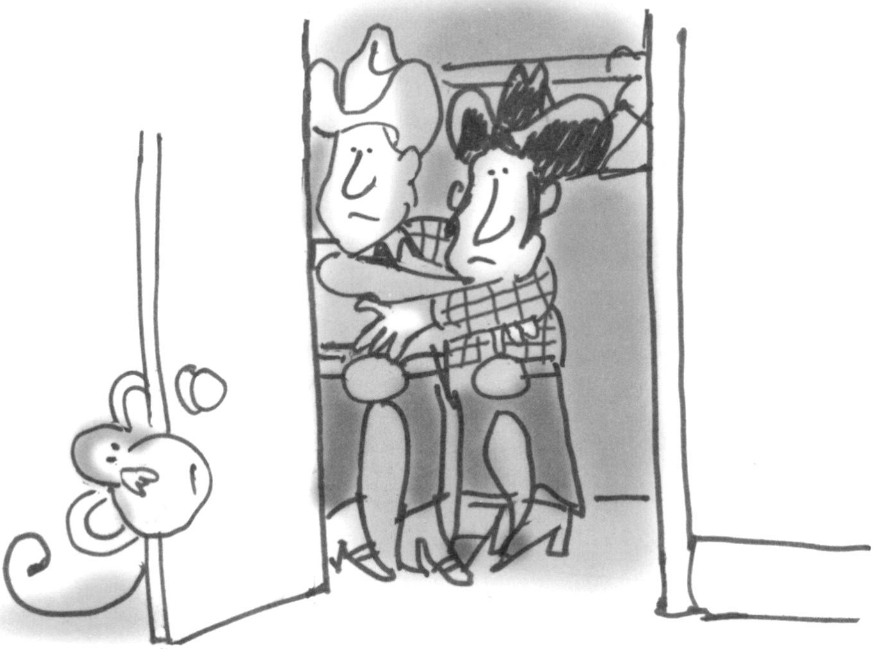

The spy monkeys searched everywhere for terrorists.

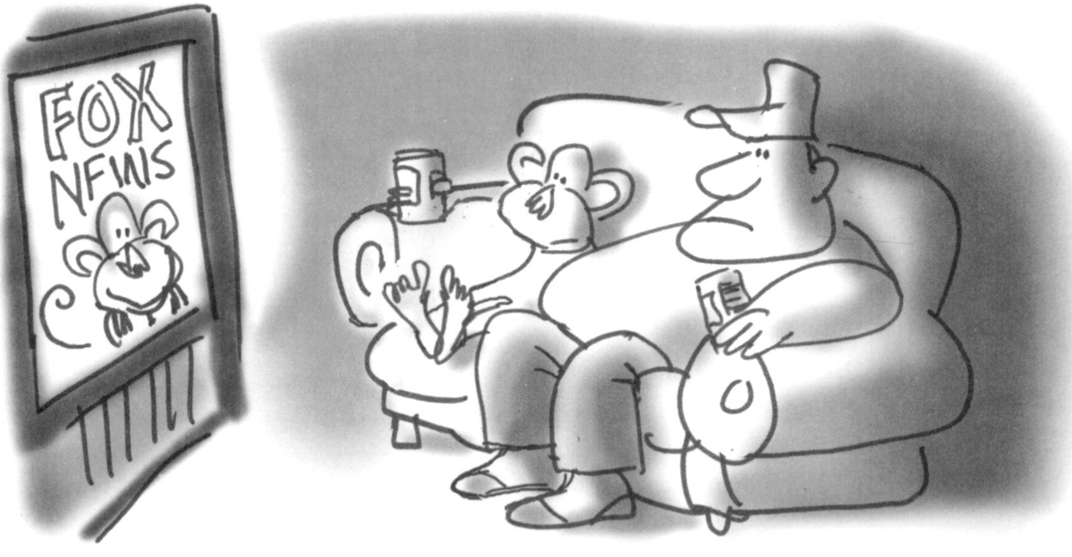
FOX
NEWS

When people thought they saw spy monkeys running loose, George called a press conference to say that those people should not trust their eyes. They should trust him.

"There is no such thing as spy monkeys," said George. "Besides, I would never, ever, ever allow hypothetical spy monkeys to spy on Americans . . . even if there were them.

"And even if I did, only people who were terrorists with something to hide would have to worry."

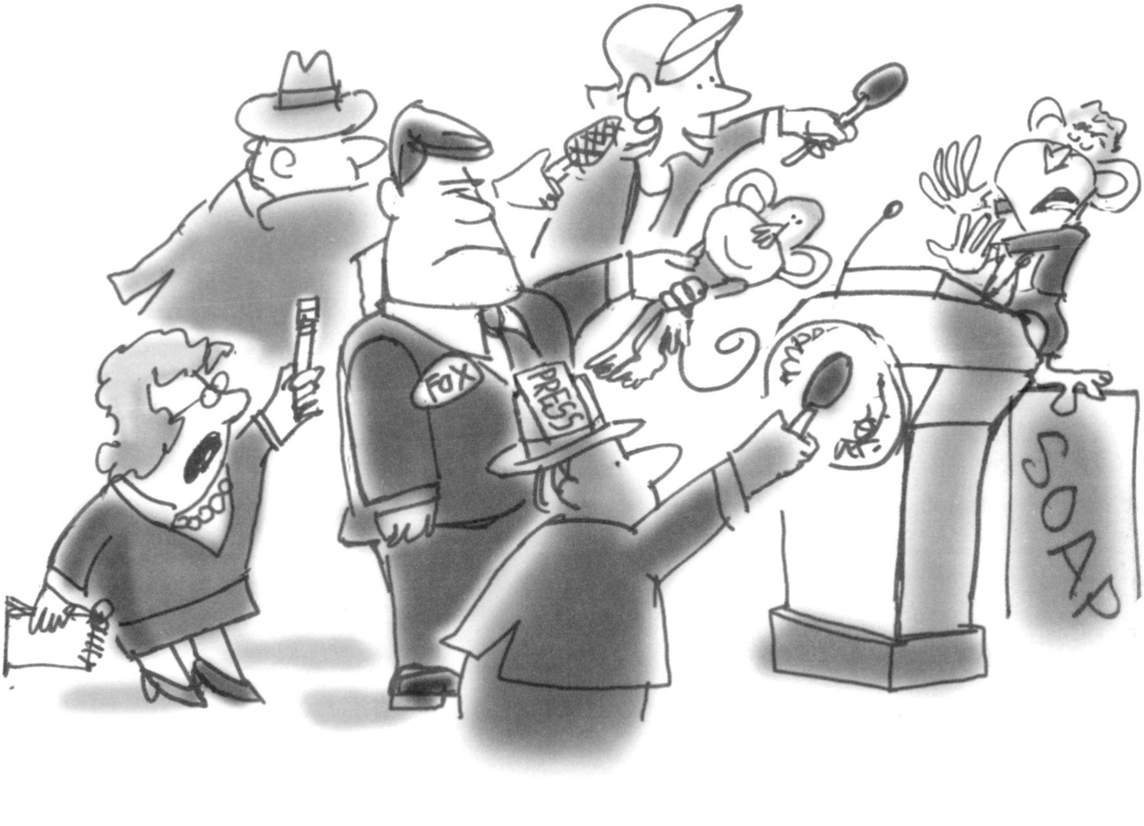
FOX
PRESS
SOAP

Meanwhile, Winston wrote strongly worded memos of protest and drank lattes.

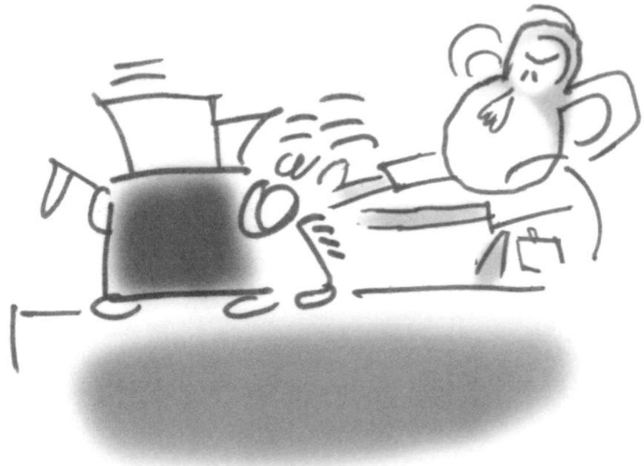

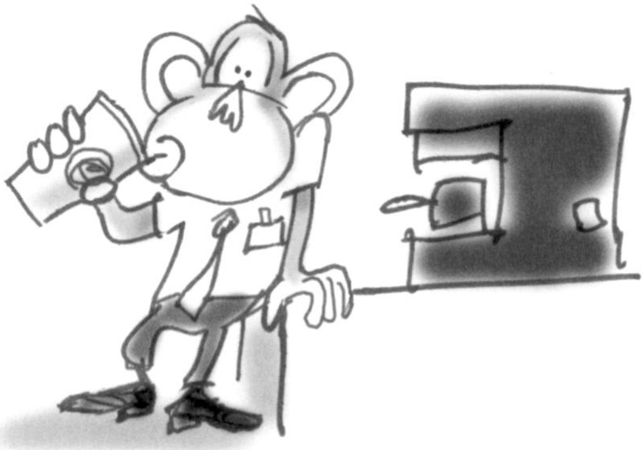

When nobody paid attention to his memos, he made them into hats.

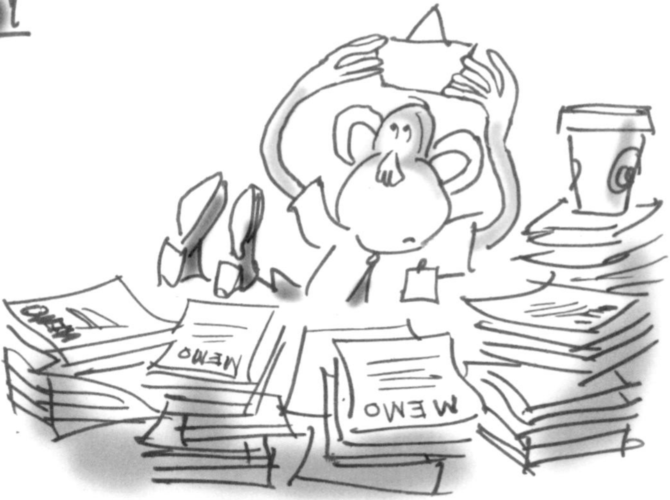

Winston made lots of hats.

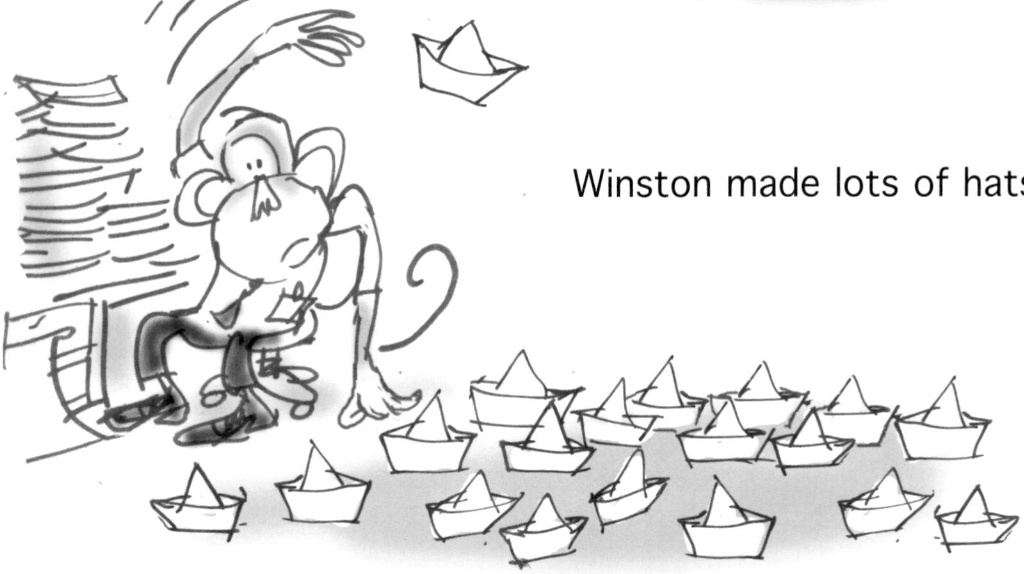

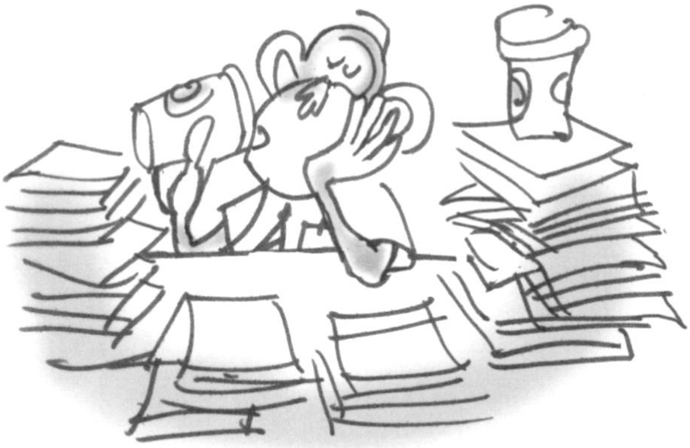

Winston drank
lots of lattes.

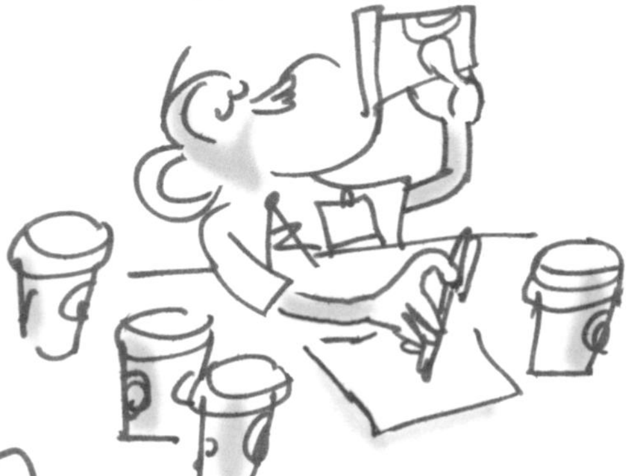

Pretty soon Winston
realized he had to
go . . .

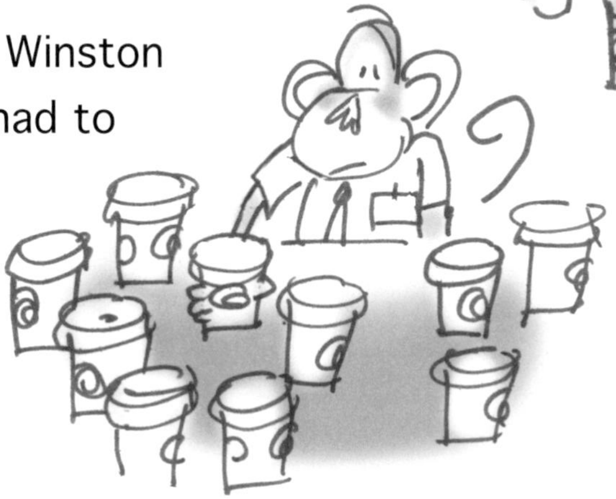

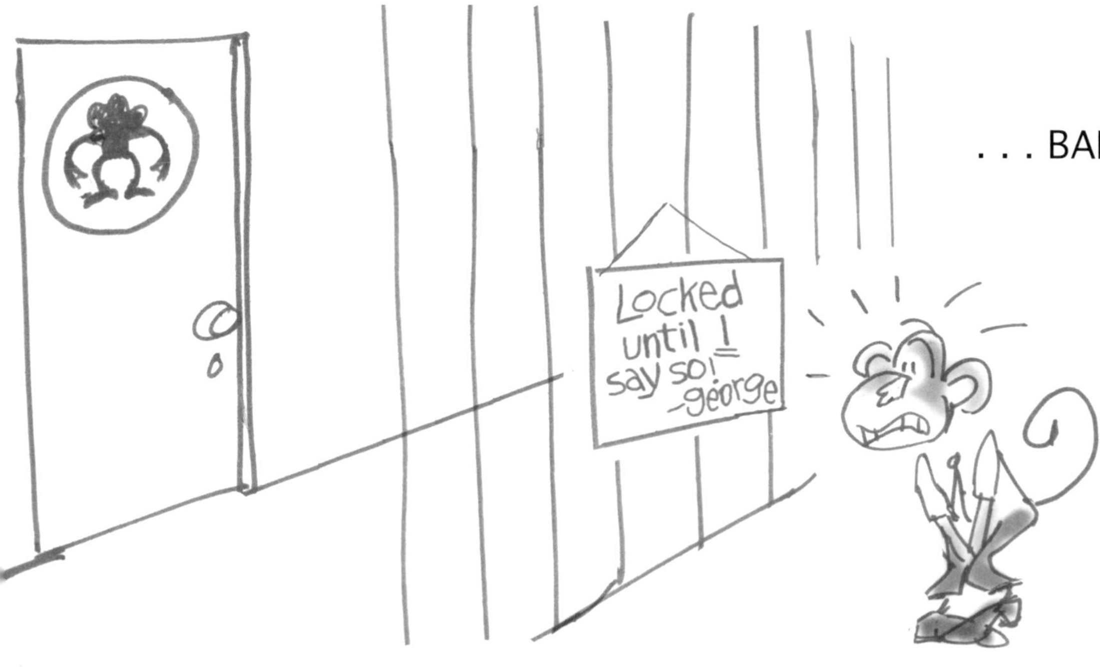
Locked until I say so! -george

. . . BAD!

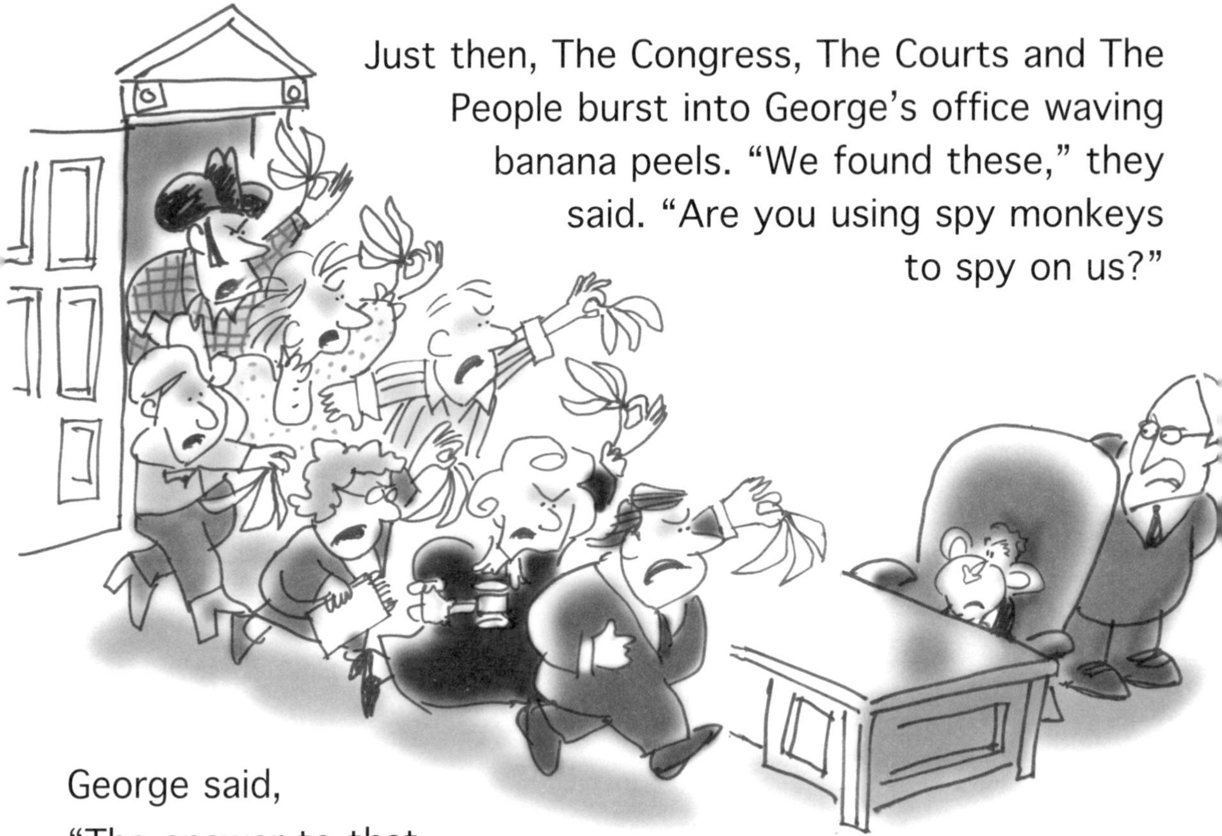

Just then, The Congress, The Courts and The People burst into George's office waving banana peels. "We found these," they said. "Are you using spy monkeys to spy on us?"

George said,
"The answer to that
is not the business of The Congress.
It is not the business of The Courts.
It is not the business of
The People . . .

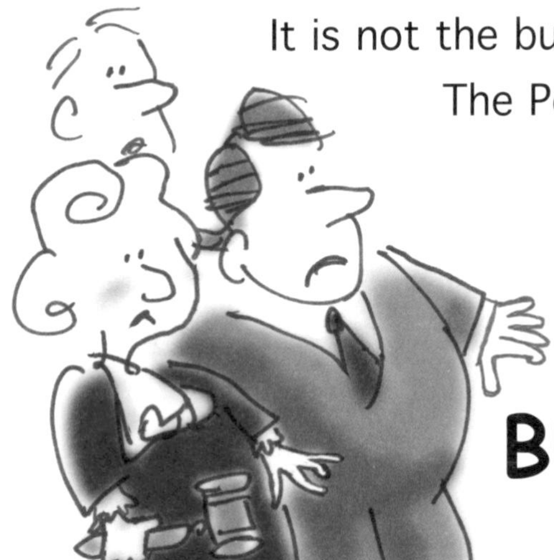

"IT IS MONKEY BUSINESS!"

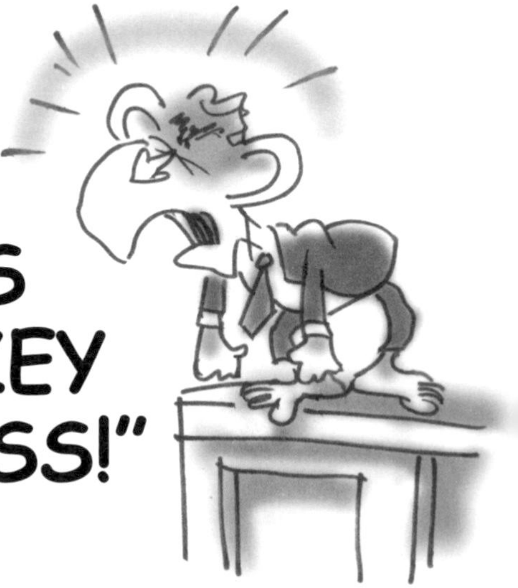

"But it *is* our business," they said. "You owe us the truth. What about our Bill of Rights? What about America being a beacon of liberty and freedom to the rest of the world? What about human rights and dignity? Isn't America all about standing for the individual against tyranny and oppression? Shouldn't we care more about preserving the ideals that make us different from the terrorists instead of becoming like them?"

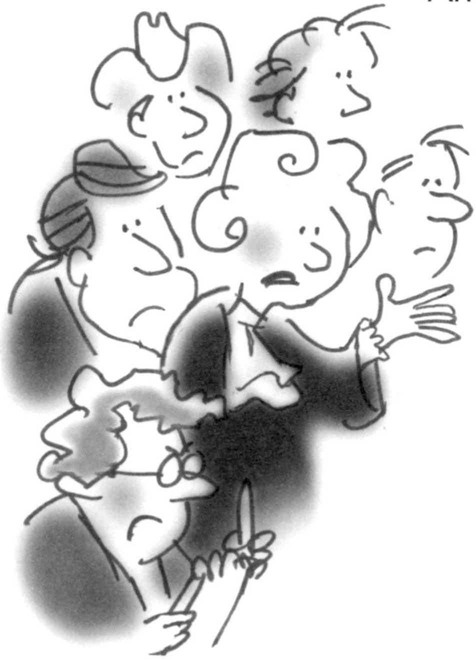

"9 -11 changed all that," said George.

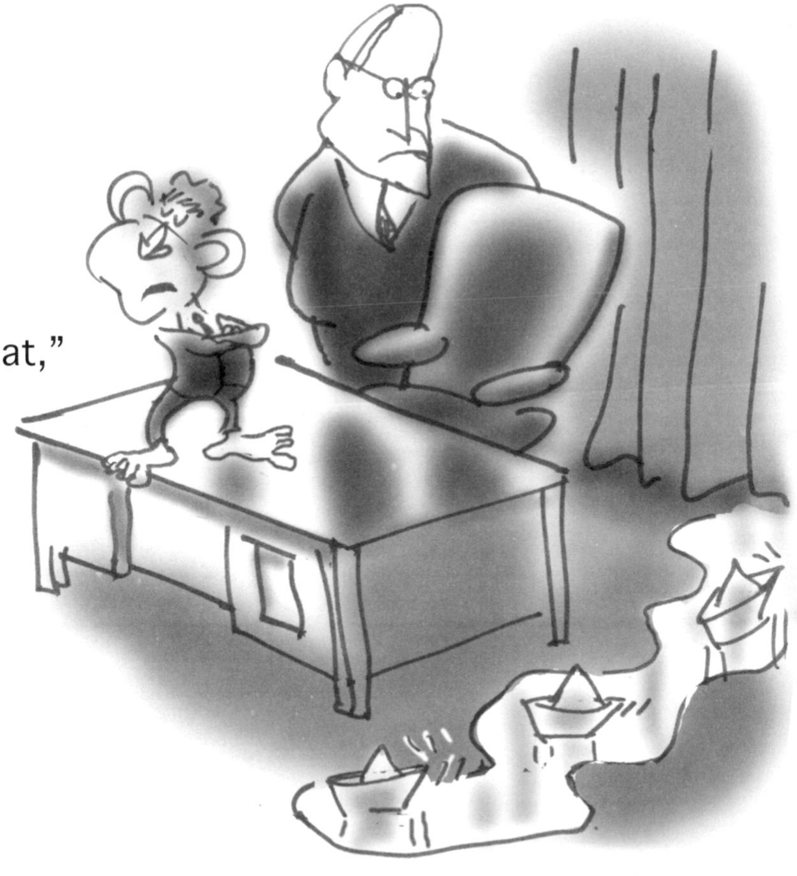

From behind the curtain a bunch of paper boats floated into George's office.

"What's this?" asked The Judge.

"That is a highly encrypted, double super-secret code that you'll never break," said The Man.

"I broke it!" said The Judge. "You just have to read it backwards."

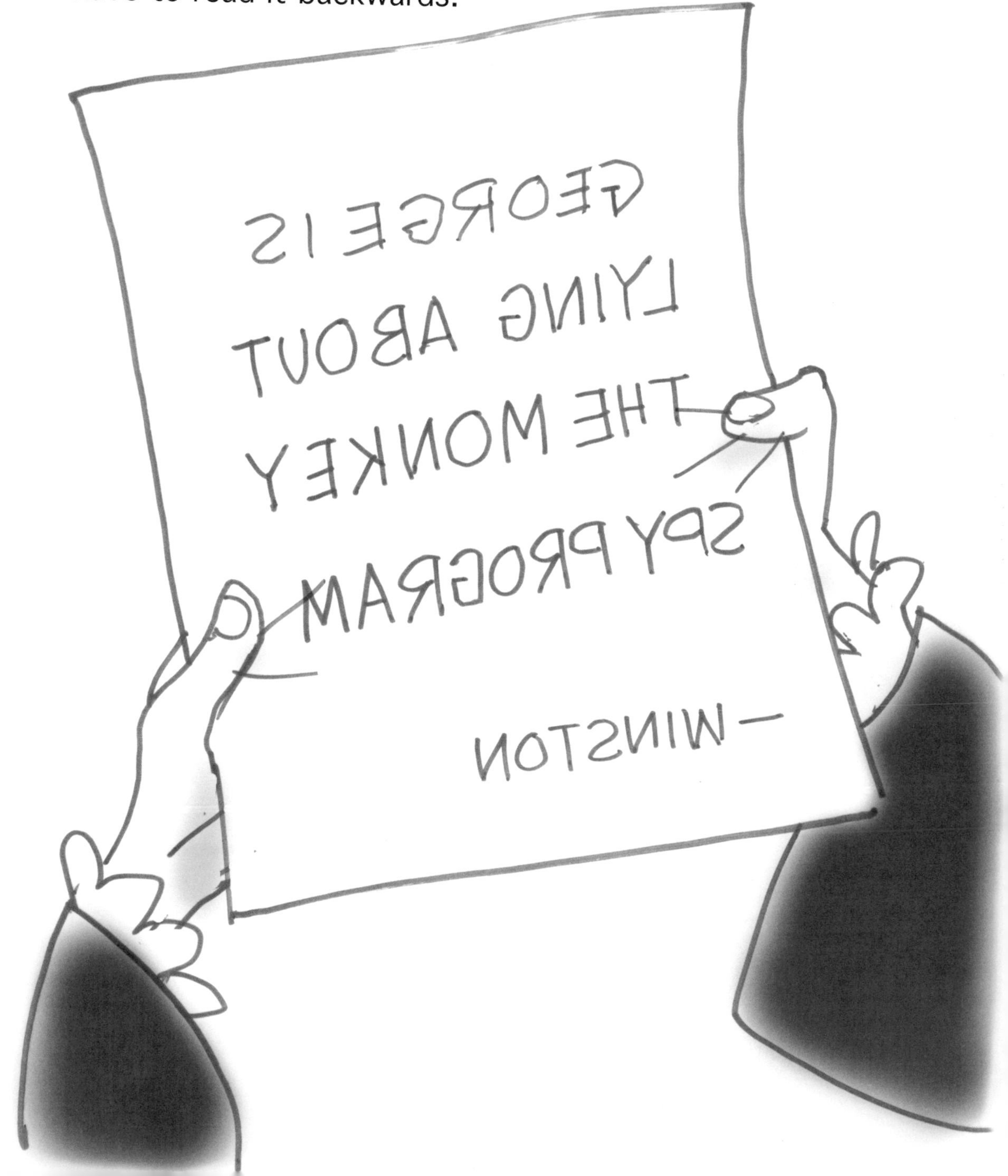
GEORGE IS
LYING ABOUT
THE MONKEY
SPY PROGRAM
—WINSTON

"Here's one that says George is an incompetent, swaggering baboon!"

"And this one says George doesn't listen to anyone!"

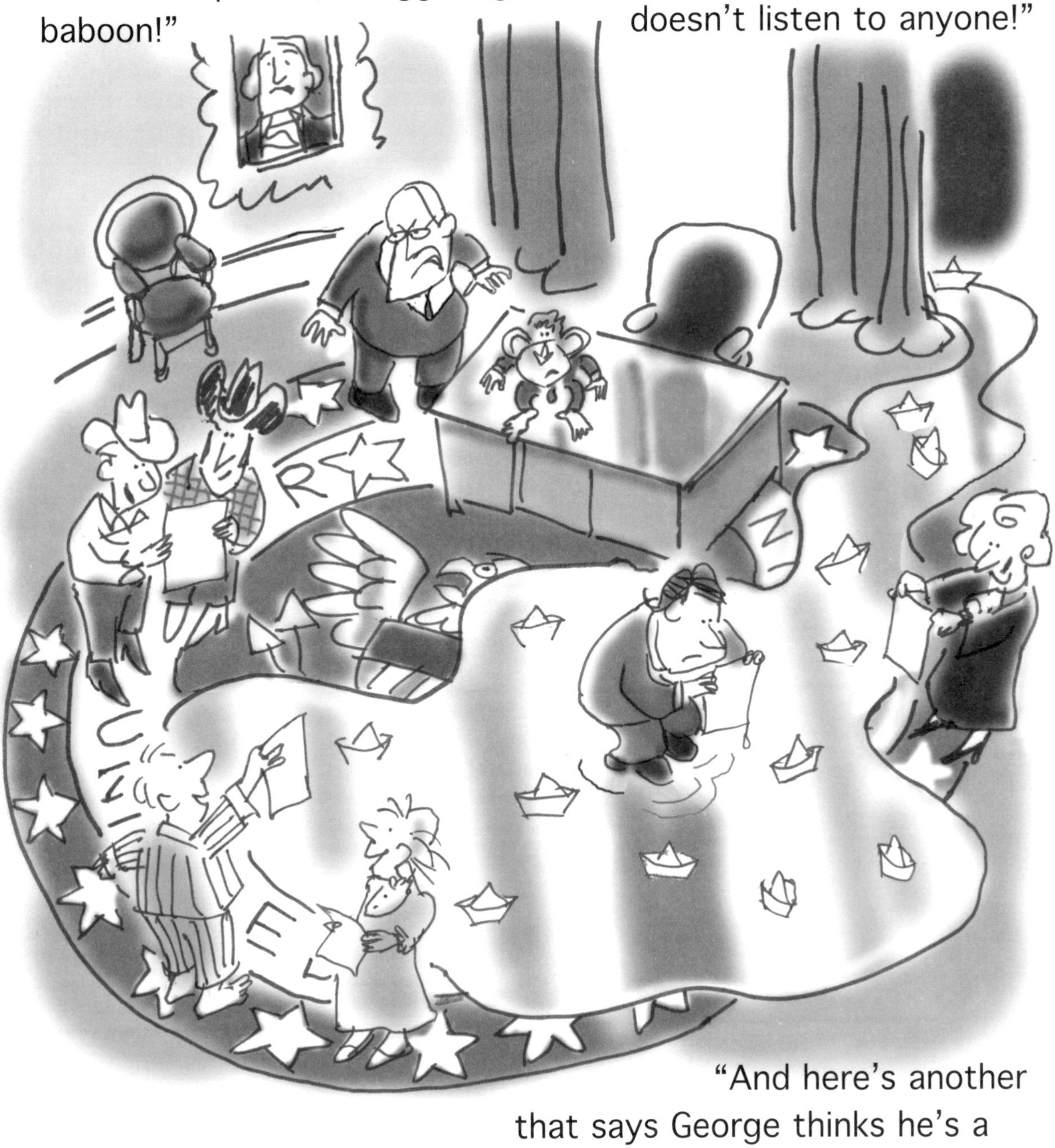

"And here's another that says George thinks he's a Ruler Monkey!"

"These are top-secret, classified documents," said The Man.

"Since when?" asked The Judge.

"Since I said so," said George.
"I am the decider and I decide the decisions."

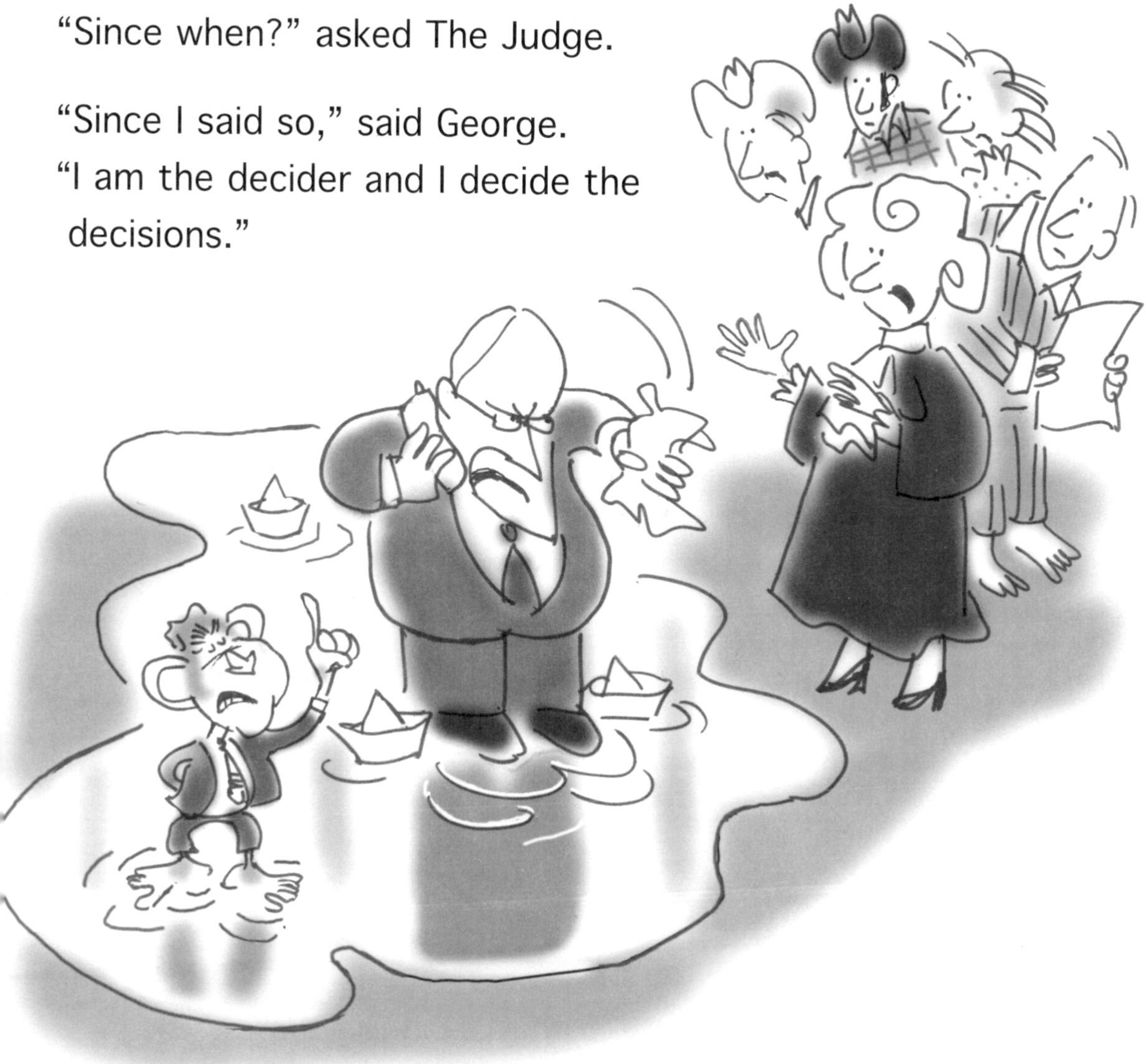

"You are all guilty of revealing sensitive information to the terrorists," The Man told them all as he dialed Homeland Security.

Later, at a secret, undisclosed location, The Man explained why The Congress, The Courts and The People were no longer against George's spy monkey program.

"I locked them up," he patiently explained.

"Isn't that against the rules?" asked George.

"You are the Ruler Monkey. You decide the rules."

"Oh, yeah," said George. "But shouldn't I have a reason anyway?"

"Okay, here is a good reason: They were reading backwards."

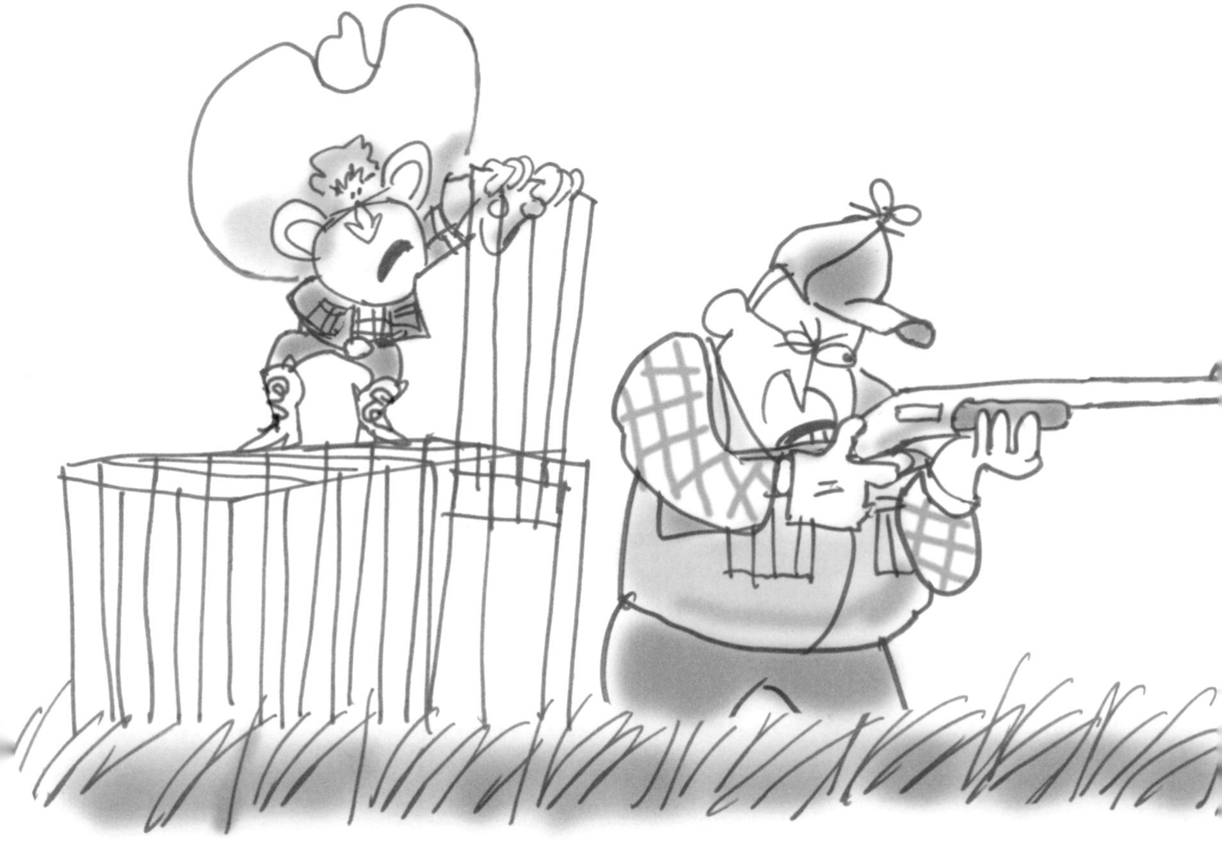

George furrowed his brow, then suddenly brightened.
"Just like the terrorists! Good thing I caught them. Does that mean we won the war against the Boxcutterivians?"
"No, there is still a lot of hard work to do," said The Man.

"Shoot!" said George.

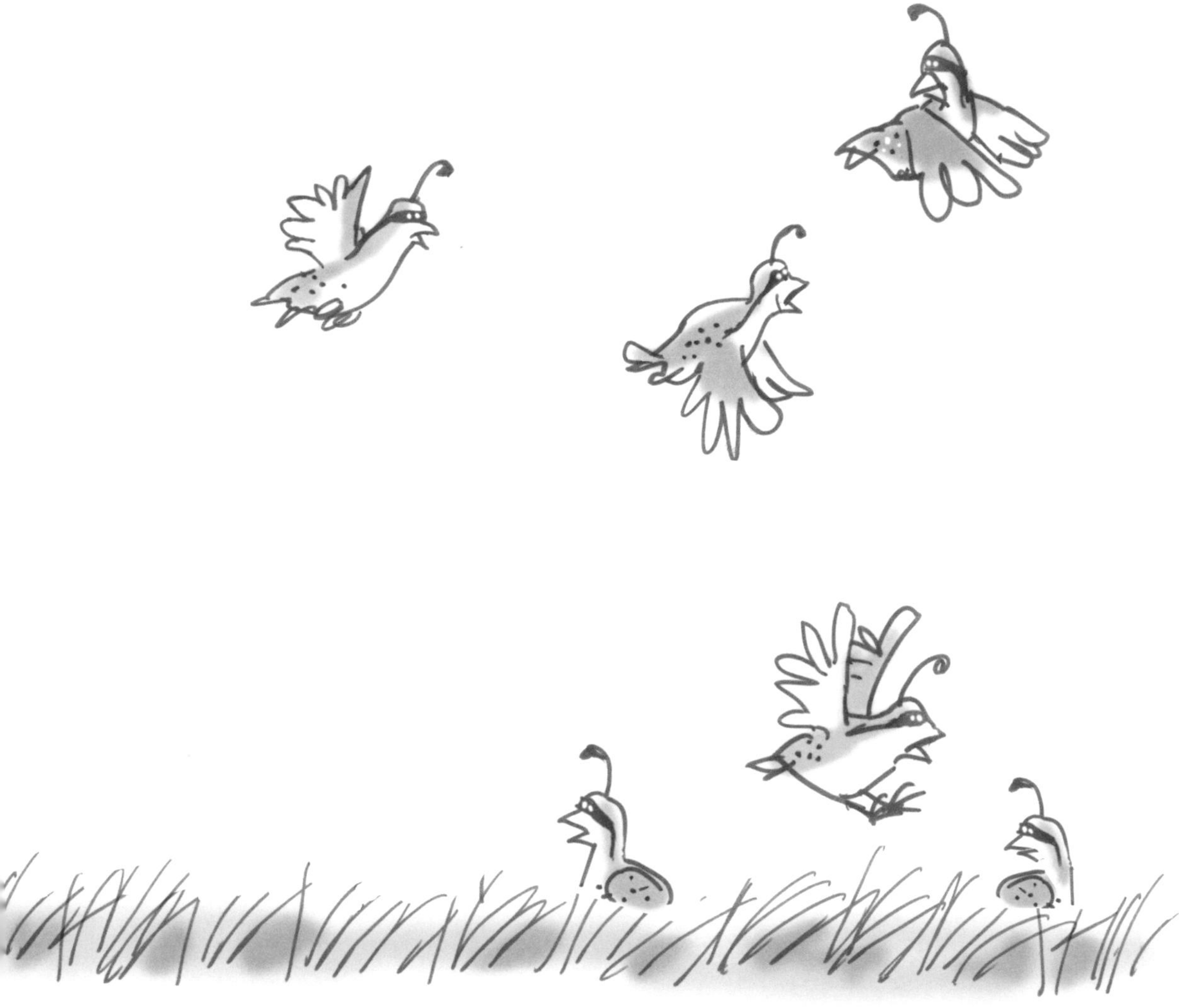

And The Man did.